NUTS & BOLTS
A blueprint for a successful illustration career

© 2010 3X3 MAGAZINE
ALL RIGHTS RESERVED. NO PART
OF THIS BOOK MAY BE REPRO-
DUCED IN ANY FORM WITHOUT
THE WRITTEN PERMISSION OF
THE COPYRIGHT HOLDER.

PUBLISHED IN THE UNITED
STATES OF AMERICA BY
3X3 THE MAGAZINE OF CONTEM-
PORARY ILLUSTRATION
244 FIFTH AVENUE, STE F269
NEW YORK NEW YORK 10001
(P) 212 591 2566
(F) 212 537 6201
WWW.3X3MAG.COM

EDITOR - CHARLES HIVELY
DESIGN - HIVELYDESIGNS
ISBN13 97809819405-4-0

Printed in Shanghai

NUTS & BOLTS
A blueprint for a successful illustration career

by CHARLES HIVELY

A PUBLICATION *of*
3X3 THE MAGAZINE *of* CONTEMPORARY ILLUSTRATION

CONTENTS

INTRODUCTION

9

HERE'S WHAT WE BELIEVE

13

THREE THINGS EVERY SUCCESSFUL ILLUSTRATOR KNOWS

20

ILLUSTRATION IS A BUSINESS

22

WEBSITES ARE MARKETING TOOLS

32

BEING VISIBLE IS ESSENTIAL

48

DO'S AND DON'TS

66

BIOGRAPHY

96

This book is a result of a 2009 visit to six universities in the United Kingdom. The response to these lectures was amazing, we saw firsthand the interest students had in learning how to approach illustration as a business. While a professor may talk about the future students are too busy completing assignments for the next class to have any thoughts about what happens once they graduate; these lectures helped point out where they were headed once class was over.

Professors, Andrew Foster and Gary Powell at Central St Martin's in London had this to say about the lecture:

"Charles Hively's candid lecture to the current cohort of MA illustration students at St Martins School of Art & Design in London in 2009, was full of energy and an in-depth knowledge about the subject of illustration.

Historical key figures, contexts of practice and the family tree of American illustration to the current day were discussed speedily to give an overview. He embraced the idea that illustration is both a global and historical subject, beyond its fashionability.

Issues were raised about the importance of draftsmanship, observational skills, intelligent creative ideas, and an awareness of professional practice was all fundamental in the pursuit of a successful illustrative career.

The very scary issue of an illustrators commercial life expectancy was also frankly highlighted, which probably scared the life out of most students. Charles' opinion in this area was a good reality check for MA students in the context of personal research and challenging boundaries.

His talk was the appropriate balance between subject knowledge, fun, quality imagery and a few scary bits. The lecture raised many student questions, which in itself says a lot. 'The lecture was followed by one of the more intense Q&A periods we'd experienced on either side of the Atlantic.' Charles reflected on the 3x3 blog.

His passion is contagious, even when you disagree with aspects of what he was actually saying. Good lectures should be informative, stimulating and a catalyst for inspiration, debate and questioning. This was a very good lecture, a pleasure to witness. We strongly recommend."

The thoughts on the following pages are a culmination of over seven years of intense observation of the illustration field and the contact that I've personally had with successful illustrators. And I'm coming at it from the perspective of a former advertising agency art director and graphic designer as well as publisher of *3x3 Magazine*. I am in a unique position to see the best and worst of illustrator's web sites and promotions as not only do I look at it now but I've been on the receiving end of promotions for most of my thirty-plus year career. On top of that I actually started out as an illustrator so I can identify with the problems illustrators face.

I hope these observations will benefit you and your career in illustration.

—CHARLES HIVELY

Here's what we Believe

Here's what we Believe
Photography cannot replicate the ideas illustrators dream up.

Here's what we Believe
No amount of digital manipulation can manufacture an idea.

Here's what we Believe
Too much of today's photography looks the same.

Here's what we Believe
Illustration looks as
different as the
illustrators themselves.

Here's what we Believe
Illustrators are as original as original gets.

Here's what we Believe
We can all take a picture.
Few of us can paint one.

Three Things Every Successful Illustrator Knows

Here's what we've found to be evident in every successful illustrator's DNA. Talent is part of it but not everything. There are a number of less-talented illustrators who are successful for these same reasons.

They approach illustration as a business.

They market their work on web sites and not blogs.

They promote themselves like crazy.

These are all inter-related, web sites and promotion are all a part of every businesses' success. But what we've found is that too many times illustrators are not treating their chosen field as a business which inhibits not only their careers but has a negative impact on the entire industry.

Our hope is that our insight can change the way illustrator's approach their careers which will benefit them as well as the rest of the illustration community.

I.
Illustration is a business.

The moment you graduate you enter the world of illustration. And whether you like it or not you are an immediate entrepreneur. Not everyone is cut out to be an entrepreneur but you have no choice. No other graduate faces going into business for themselves right out of school. Others may dream about having their own business one day but everyone except illustrators find a job working for someone else.

As an entrepreneur you certainly are afforded perks that an employee doesn't have. You can call your own shots, set your own timetables, create your own goals. But in so doing you need to have the proper mindset. You need to start looking at illustration as a business and not a hobby.

Your responsibilities include not only creating that visual solution, you're responsible for negotiating the fee, billing and collecting the fee, filing reports, paying taxes, purchasing insurance and developing marketing plans to make sure you're continually busy.

I.
Illustration is a business. You work for yourself.

I.
Illustration is a business.
You find projects.

I.
Illustration is a business. You negotiate fees.

I.
Illustration is a business.
You bill and collect.

I.
Illustration is a business. You setup accounting systems.

I.
Illustration is a business.
You file paperwork.

I.
Illustration is a business.
You pay taxes.

I.
Illustration is a business. You hire lawyers, accountants, business planners.

2.
Websites are Marketing tools.

One of the most common mistakes we see is the poor use of web sites to market an illustrator's work.

Too many are difficult or slow to load.

Too many show the work too small.

Too many make it hard to capture an image for a layout.

Too many show every piece they've ever done.

Too many have no clear personal vision.

Too many show personal sketches.

Too few show work in context.

Too few have an easy way to contact the artist.

Too few are easy to navigate.

2.
Websites are Marketing tools.
Blogs are not Marketing tools.

There is a trend lately where illustrators have bypassed a web site and have gone to blogs or Flicker or YouTube to market their work. While all of these are important as a part of publicizing your work, no successful illustrator has forgone a web site.

Web sites show work that will engage the viewer in the hopes of landing a commission. Blogs should be used for communicating to a select audience of acquaintances or friends and not to a new client. Once you've established a relationship with an art director, certainly invite them to see your blog.

Blogs are good for showing process but few art directors or art buyers have the time or patience to scroll down your blog to find images you've done. And your best work may not be what you're showing first. The best web sites give the viewer just what they need to make a decision on your work. Making it easy for them at this point is critical to getting work. Forgoing it just for the sake of money or expediency is not a good approach.

2.
Websites are Marketing tools.
Websites are dead-simple to navigate.

You have less than ten seconds to attract an art director's attention; if minutes are spent trying to upload your site then you've just lost a sale even before the work has been seen.

Art directors are busy individuals, they have a lot on their plate. A typical day may involve multiple meetings, reading creative briefs, developing campaigns, presenting concepts and refining work or production. So you need to make your web site easy to open and easy to see all your work. Remember your job is to show the work, not create a dazzling site full of bells and whistles.

The best sites are those that allow an art director to move their cursor across your small thumbnails which then enlarge the image to a size that is at least 455 pixels wide. Larger if your work is complex.

Pop-up windows are a no-no. Making the art director close one image to open another is verboten. Flash sites slow down both loading and capturing images.

2.
Websites are Marketing tools.
Websites create name recognition.

Your url and email address should reinforce your name making it easier for art directors to remember you.

An art director may forget who they commissioned two months ago, so every time you contact them or send your mailers or email blasts make sure your name is repeated in as many places as possible.

Make your web site address easy to remember: firstandlastname.com. Make your email address your first name at your web address: firstname@firstandlastname.com. Don't be clever with either your web or email address. Using a hotmail or gmail for your email address says you're not a professional.

If your full name is too long use your first name plus the word "art" or "illustrates". Don't resort to something like: marylovesart@marylovestomakeart.com. There are too many Mary's out there so as an art director I need to associate you with your full name. Name recognition counts.

2.
Websites are
Marketing tools.
Websites show only
your best work.

You must be ruthless when determining which images you show on your website.

Don't rely on friend's judgement or your spouses or significant other. Seek out a professional whom you respect to look at your site and ask them to critique the work. You want an honest, non-biased opinion.

Find your best piece and judge every other image against that image. Look at your images in a mirror or upside down—many times that will point out flaws.

Remember you will be judged by your weakest piece not your best piece. Why? Because an art director will always hope to get your best work but will not accept anything less than your weakest piece.

And it's a matter of degrees, the weakest piece can't be light years from your best piece, the quality of all the images needs to be at a high-level.

2.
Websites are Marketing tools.
Websites promote third-party endorsements.

If you've just completed an assignment from *The New York Times* you want to shout about it. You want to include not only the image but also the date it ran and the art director you worked with.

Remember you're working in a relatively small community; the fact that one art director has used you can lead to fellow art directors calling you for their next job.

You need to think of yourself like a brand. You're new to the market, how do you establish your reputation? Think about any new product you've seen, how did they promote themselves to you?

You're not any different than that product or service; third-party endorsements go a long way to alleviate any misconceptions or fears they may have about you and your work.

Too many illustrators feel they're giving away an important contact information by sharing the name of the art director—that's simply unjustified.

2.
Websites are Marketing tools.
Websites allow easy ways to select and save.

One of the reasons you have a web site is for art directors or art buyers to see images they can use.

Most will need to somehow show your work to someone else or even use it for rough layouts to show their boss or a client.

Making it easy to copy your work is important. There is one caveat, you want to specify on your site that work may not be used without your written permission but that it is permissible to use the 72 dpi image as part of a layout for presentation purposes only.

Make it easy for the art director. By using control + click it's the simplest way for the art director to capture the image they need.

Flash sites can make it more time-consuming for an art director to select an image. Adding steps to capturing the image could very well lead to a lost sale. Keep it simple and you have a better shot at getting an assignment.

2.
Websites are Marketing tools.
Websites are constantly being updated.

Hopefully you'll have methods in place for advertising and promoting your site so art directors or art buyers will want to come back to your site often.

Be sure to upload new images immediately after a job is completed.

Make note of any new awards you've received, new commissions you're working on or any new exhibits you'll be participating in.

You want to look busy to anyone who visits your site.

A neglected site may send the wrong message, while you may be too busy to update your site it actually will come off as you're not busy at all.

Set aside a day each month to update your site.

3.
Being visible is essential.

The one thing most successful illustrators have in common is they are all visible.

Whether it's in the media.

Or in a gallery show.

Or in an annual.

Or in a directory.

Or an email blast.

Or a mailing.

They are constantly out there promoting their work.

It can be said that only about 10 percent of your time is spent creatively, the rest of the time is spent on the business side of illustration and there's no more important part than promotion.

3.
Being visible is essential.
You're everywhere.

You want to be seen in as many places as possible. Think of any new product or service that's come out, you see them here and then there and then on the shelf. It seems like they've been around forever and yet they're a brand new product. You're no different.

And like a brand, you'll need to be seen at least three times before you've even made the slightest impression. That could mean mailing three postcards or three email blasts over a short period of time. But definitely one shot is not enough to make any impression; if it does then it's rare.

So you want to be seen in as many places as physically and financially possible. And don't just seek out the free spots to be in, spend some cold hard cash advertising and promoting yourself. Successful illustrators spend at least 20 percent of their income on promotion.

By promoting yourself you look successful. Look successful. Be successful.

3.
Being visible is essential.
You enter every show.

Too many young illustrators feel that entering shows is a waste of time and money but consider this: the judges who judge these shows are the same people who commission illustration. An entry fee is a small price to pay for getting in front of them. And it's been proven that work has come from just being entered in a show—you don't always have to be a winner to get work.

Judging is subjective and in most shows it takes a majority of judge's votes to be accepted into the show. That could mean that two out of four judges may like your work but it doesn't have enough votes to get in. But if they like your work they'll find out who entered and you may end up getting a call.

Not all shows are created equal. You want to make sure you know who is judging your work and make sure art directors, creative directors, art buyers or graphic designers are on that judging panel. If not, pass.

3.
Being visible is essential. You show your work in directories.

Too many directories are old-hat. And admittedly directories are not the resource they once were. Why? Because they have taken the pay-to-play approach. They are not curated, anyone who has the financial means can buy a page. So the work is a mixed bag, some good work, but too many mediocre pieces which turns off an art director.

I used to love directories but over the past ten years they've been used more as doorstops than a resource.

There are exceptions—touting our horn 3x3's is a curated directory. We only invite those who have entered our shows, been in our magazine or we have discovered online. We're highly selective. And we're inexpensive. Where others cost thousands of dollars as page, ours are in the hundreds.

So use directories as a way to get the word out about your work in an environment with the best illustrators. It will help you. It will help the industry.

3.
Being visible is essential. You show your work in galleries.

The lines are blurring between illustration and fine art; illustrators can be seen one day in a magazine or animated spot and the next weekend be displayed on the gallery wall. In most instances the images don't look any different wherever they're seen.

Illustrators would once have to make the work more "fine art" to hang in a gallery, no more. The work we see on their site is now viewed in the same context and respect as fine art.

There are numerous galleries who welcome illustrators; who promote the sale of illustration. The format may be larger or the medium may be different but it embodies the heart and soul of the artist.

This new attitude helps illustrators create a name for themselves and adds immensely to their visibility.

The audience is also broader when an artist is featured in a gallery going beyond the art director and maybe even as far as to the ultimate client level.

3.
Being visible is essential.
Your work is in recognizable media.

Being seen in publications that have wide appeal is important to building the reputation of an illustrator. Not only being seen in as many places as possible but being seen in prestigious magazines and books helps build that reputation.

Building your reputation is important to sustaining your career. There are only a handful of artists who have had a successful thirty year career. The average career only lasts seven to ten years with most of that time being spent getting recognized. Unfortunately tastes change, trends end and at some point you'll need to reinvent yourself. You may need to go back to school or take a sabbatical away from work to find the new you. As with any brand you will peak and then decline. Adjusting to that circumstance and coming out again with a fresh voice is just half the fun of being an illustrator.

Reestablishing yourself will not be as difficult as your first time, working in established media with art directors you've developed relationships with will help enable the transition.

3.
Being visible is essential.
You promote yourself
on a regular basis.

We did a survey of 200 illustrators asking them how and when they promoted and how much they allocated to their promotion budget.

The results were disheartening. For the most part illustrators did one promotion a year, spent no more than $500 and did the promotion around the holidays.

Photographers spend thousands of dollars promoting themselves to art directors. Most brands spend millions. How can anyone conceive of building a business spending so little? Our survey found successful illustrators spent upwards of $4000 a year on promotion.

Do not promote yourself during the holidays, it's in poor taste. Certainly if you've established a relationship with an art director send them a card, otherwise promote every other time but then. You should be promoting your work at the minimum, once a month.

Select one day every month and send out something. Be consistent. Be constant.

3.
Being visible is essential.
Mailers.
Emails. With links.

Mix it up. Send an email blast one month, a post card the next, a personal project in the form of a booklet or comic the next, a mini poster, a self-published book. Keep it varied.

And it can be as simple as sending out an email announcing your latest project with a direct link to your site.

It could be an email blast that shows your latest project. Remember to credit the art director and client you did the project for within the email.

When it comes to postcards make sure the image is relevant. As an art director I kept the images that solved a problem in a unique way. Give yourself a problem to solve and use that image as your promotion. Don't send out a piece just because it's your favorite.

Make it personal, either a one-off image or at the very least dress-up the envelope to make it eye-catching. I have an entire collection of artist's envelopes.

3.
Being visible is essential. Develop your own mailing lists.

You don't want to just buy a list and send it out, you want to select the art directors or clients you want to work for.

Scour magazines and books, find art directors who work on projects that fit your unique vision. Get contact information from the masthead.

Develop your own database which include the proper contact person with mailing and email address.

This list may be no larger than 100 and of that list you should have a hot list of 25 art directors that you really want to work for who receive special, one-off mailings in addition to the ones you're sending out.

Subscribe to a list service like Adbase which allows you to customize your list.

Develop several lists and send out different mailings depending on who the audience is.

Do's & Don'ts.

The following are some thoughts about how to approach your career as a young illustrator.

What we find is that when a graduate enters the marketplace they are so anxious to get work that they sometimes ignore the basic principles of the business. This is neither good for their career nor for the industry as a whole.

And as soon as someone knows you're new to the field they'll try to take advantage of you. Either by the projects they give you, the money they budget or the time they give you to complete the assignment. You must educate yourself quickly about fees and timetables to find out what is fair and reasonable.

Our list of do's and don'ts are a direct result of our constant observations of web sites, artist portfolios, meetings with student groups and with established artists who have shared their experiences in the marketplace.

Do be original.
Don't copy.

While you may think it's expeditious to copy a current style your best bet for the long haul is to develop your own personal vision.

It's okay to be influenced by another artist but any direct resemblance to their work that may result in confusion should be avoided. You don't want to be known as a copycat, be yourself.

While there are art directors who will purposefully seek out those who copy a style that artist is being sought out not because they're unique but usually because they can't afford the original.

No one says it's easy developing your own unique style and certainly you may experience difficulty in arriving at something that is commercially successful. It takes time to be original. But don't forsake your work just to make a fast buck.

Trends fade; you want to develop something that will last and that is truly yours.

Do be professional.
Don't be a prima donna.

You'd be surprised by how many times a student or recent graduate will tell me that they're just a student or new to the field. Remember the moment you step outside that classroom into the real world you're expected to be a professional.

You want to make sure you do everything in your power to come across as if you have been in the field for years, not months.

You want to work with art directors not against them. You want to be flexible with deadlines and money. And you want to listen to constructive criticism. And this should be your tact from day one and last throughout your career.

No one wants to work with an asshole, and perhaps when you've made a huge name for yourself you can be a bit of a prima donna, after all we don't have to like you to love your work. But in the beginning, stay lovable.

Do be outgoing.
Don't be a recluse.

Illustration is a solitary career. The large portion of illustrators work by themselves, usually at home. While the commute to the office is a short one there are certain disadvantages to working on your own. Having your studio at home will be cheaper but be sure to augment your live/work arrangement with social activities that get you out of the house.

Join a club.

Make friends.

Go for a walk.

Take up a hobby.

Sometimes these outside activities actually aid the creative process.

I've found there's little use sitting by the phone waiting for it to ring or for the chime in your email inbox. Get out of the studio. It'll do you good.

Do join clubs.
Don't just join the Society
of Illustrators or AOI.

A common mistake illustrators make is to only join an illustration organization.

It's easy to understand why. Your friends are there. It's a group you feel welcome in. It's a good place to meet artists you admire. It's a comfortable environment.

Your friends at the Society or the Association of Illustrators are important but you're not going to get any work from them. They may alert you as to who not to work for but they're not a source for work.

As the saying goes, go where the fishes are. Join your local art directors club, graphic designer or publication designer organization or even the advertising club. Remember these are the people who will commission your work. These are the people you want to meet.

And when you join, volunteer. Make sure you are a well-recognized member and be sure you're also recognized as an illustrator.

Do take ADs to lunch. Don't just hang with illustrators.

In my career as an ad agency art director photographers would constantly be inviting me out for lunch. And in all my career never once did an illustrator. And I'm not alone, it's rare that you see an illustrator inviting an art director to lunch.

I understand that illustrators are most likely introverts. And I understand why it may be difficult to pick up the phone and invite someone to lunch. Maybe just start off with coffee or invite them to your gallery opening or studio open house. Break the ice somehow.

But sooner or later just make the offer, many times they won't have the time to meet up but at least you've shown an interest.

Remember it's not a time to be showing your work or necessarily talking about your latest project—you're trying to get to know them on a more personal level.

Building long-lasting relationships with art directors can help your career last a lot longer.

Do support the community. Don't just promote yourself.

We've talked alot about promotion but it's also important to support the illustration community.

Join the SOI or AOI. Volunteer your time and talents.

Enter their shows. Serve on juries.

Be an advocate for the illustration community. Talk with your friends outside the business about the importance of illustration.

Join online groups. Be responsive to queries, offer feedback.

Subscribe to industry publications. Buy the annuals. Buy books on illustration and illustrators.

And subscribe to all the publications that you either want your work to be seen in or have been in. The subscription is a small price to pay for supporting those who are supporting you.

Do be selective.
Don't take every job.

There is a tendency to take every job you are called in for—not a good idea.

Make sure the job is something you can do. Something that you'll enjoy doing.

Make sure you can do it within the time allotted.

Make sure you can bring something fresh to the table.

Don't take the job just because of a big budget. Or because you've not had any jobs recently. Make sure it's a good fit for you and for your client.

There's nothing worse than taking a job and doing it poorly. Or delivering it late. Art directors have better longterm memories of those who fail than for those who succeed.

You won't get many second-chances, if any.

Do bid fairly.
Don't undercut a pro.

Starting out you'll be under a lot of pressure to produce, to land that first job and you may think you have to pull out all the stops to get it.

Be careful. As someone new to the industry there will be those who will try to take advantage of you. They'll suggest that by doing their project for free it will be a good way to promote your work. That's rarely the case.

As for paying jobs, one sure thing is that you won't be able to charge what someone whose been in the business longer can charge. Don't be naive about what the cost should be, just charge a bit less.

Certainly don't low-ball your fee or give it away just to get the job. It's not beneficial to you, it's not fair to your fellow illustrators and it damages the industry.

If you're not sure what to charge ask an established illustrator. Keep in mind editorial budgets are mostly set while advertising budgets are flexible and will depend on where and how your art is used.

Do research.
Don't just make
something up.

Always remember you're a visual problem solver. To solve the problem you first have to know what the problem is.

You need to know more about the job than just the size and deadline. Even if it's an editorial job you should at least look at previous issues or if you have the time read other work by the author.

In advertising jobs you need to know as much about the client, the product or service you're working on as possible. Research them online. Always ask for more information if you're unsure about the problem. And make sure you know where it's going to be seen, i.e. what section of the magazine.

Find out who the competition is, what kind of art are they using?

What I've found is that the solution comes from within the problem itself. It's not something that you just dream up. It's based on something tangible and honest.

Do lots of sketches. Don't just do your first idea.

The minute you get the job the wheels in your brain start turning. And you may arrive at the perfect solution right there and then. But it is highly unlikely.

When you're being briefed on the project always have a pen and pad handy—write down the specifics of the project, don't doodle ideas at this point. Make sure you are clear on what the project is before you end the conversation.

Once you start the project, sketch. Don't use the computer, use a pencil or pen and paper. Write down words, phrases—make it a point of departure. Sketching helps our brain start to work. And keep it small—that's why they're called thumbnails.

My old boss told me I needed to spend hours working on an idea just to get the shit out of my system. When you're new to the game it does take hours to arrive at a truly unique answer. And yes, you might come back to that very first idea but it's more likely that a newer, fresher idea will emerge.

Do make a website.
Don't just use your blog.

It takes time and sometimes some cold hard cash to develop a really good web site. On the other hand it just takes a couple of minutes to get a blog up and running. Don't make a blog your default just because it doesn't cost anything. Build a full-blown web site.

Blogs are great for communicating with friends but remember the art director who is looking to hire you isn't your friend, yet.

Make it easy for them to find your work. Don't have them scrolling down an endless stream of images and text to look at your work.

Sure, have a link on your site to your blog. And certainly invite the art director whose become a client to view your blog but not until then.

A web site means you're a professional. Just using a blog does not and forcing an art director to settle for just your blog is not helpful and may be perceived as being a bit arrogant.

Do be ruthless.
Don't show everything
you've ever done.

You wouldn't believe how many websites I see that have over a hundred images on them. It's like they're showing everything they've ever done. No art director has the time to see all those images.

While there's a tendency to show more images on a site the rule must be to show only the best images. If you only have six really good images show six images. Quantity doesn't count, quality does.

And constantly update your site. At least once a month you should be adding and changing out images.

And don't show sketches, life drawing, landscapes, still-lives or the like unless they have some commercial application. Showing what you like to do in your off-hours sends a confusing message to your audience.

An art director will spend just a few seconds on your site, make sure they only see your best work. They will make snap judgements on as few as one or two images.

Do subscribe to print.
Don't just rely on the web.

Sure getting your information, news or entertainment off the web is fast and easy but don't forget that your work primarily appears in print. In magazines, newspapers. Transit posters. In editorial or advertising. On labels. Or bookcovers.

It's important that you support print in its many forms.

We've all heard that print is supposedly dying but keep in mind when television arrived radio didn't disappear. But we're not helping the situation when we who make our living in print fail to support print. Subscribe to the publications your work is seen in, or you want to be seen in.

The real issue is that more and more we're taking free content for granted which unfortunately will lead to less acceptance for paying for art. If we're not paying for text why pay for art?

Resist the temptation to get everything from a source which gives back so little monetarily.

Do subscribe to 3x3. Don't forget to enter our shows.

It's important to support our efforts here at 3x3 as we are the leading advocate for contemporary illustration. We're doing our part to build more respect for illustration and awareness of illustrators through our publications, books and blog.

We believe strongly in what we're doing; we're passionate about illustration and see a bright future for our industry. But building respect takes a concerted effort on everyone's part. From professors to students, emerging artists to well-established ones. Each and every one of you represent the industry as a whole. Please never forget that.

Supporting our publications and annual shows means we have a larger voice in promoting illustration. We can do more projects that get the word out about illustration. We'll only be as successful as you help make us.

A subscription or a show entry or being in our directory is a small price to pay to help promote illustration and illustrators.

CHARLES HIVELY *Biography*

His background began in illustration. "I was always drawing something as a kid. My favorites were always heads and trees. That led my parents to enroll me in the Famous Artists correspondence school. I have to admit I never finished the course but they were pleased enough of my work to show my work in a number of their in-house magazine issues which lead to a number of freelance assignments."

"I got this job selling art supplies right out of high school, it was a great opportunity to meet art directors and designers and eventually led to a full-time job in a television station's art department. Of course, I didn't get to do illustration at first, just loads of cutting mats, photo processing, and handsetting type for camera cards. But before I headed off to college I got an opportunity to do the front cover of the local paper's CBS Fall Preview section which was quite the coup."

Influenced by the work of Alan Cober, Bernie Fuchs, Franklin McMahon, and Mark English, Hively continued to experiment with different mediums. "I've tried every medium there is including airbrush, which lasted about a day, but I always come back to pen and ink." Thinking he would continue working at a television station when he arrived at college, he approached one but found no openings, fortunately across the street was an ad agency that was looking for a production artist. Again, no illustration for the first couple of years until the need for a spot illustration came up and Hively jumped at the chance. But suffering from a terrible cold he was convinced his odd drawing would never see the light of day, but as it happened it was a success which led to many more assignments including numerous covers for the local business magazine, advertising, brochures and posters.

He enjoyed the professional life of an illustrator while still going to school. After graduating he formed his first advertising agency, "I wanted to combine my love for illustration with concept and design and we became noted for our stylish advertising. Our clients were all about our same age so they appreciated our thinking." Awards came to the agency and a chance to work in a larger market prompted Hively to move and join a bigger agency where he continued to promote the use of illustration, even contributing his own work to projects. He also got to work with some of the best illustrators in the country including Seymour Chwast, Ed Sorel, Charles Saxon, *The New Yorker* cartoonists, Lou Myers and Jean Michel Folon. "I could ape the style of almost every artist for the comp phase and would sometimes have trouble convincing clients to use the "real thing," but in all situations I was successful and thoroughly enjoyed working with illustrators."

Hively still draws for his personal enjoyment but after owning another agency and working for *Graphis* as a co-publisher Hively enjoys this new avenue. "At *3x3* I get to look at illustrators from all over the world and invite them to be a part of something new, it's truly exciting and I don't even consider it work."

NUTS & BOLTS NOTES